What Our Readers Have Said...

"Although I consider myself a seasoned sales professional, it is helpful to have past learning's refreshed. The books were also beneficial because of the information concerning 'trends' in the sales relationship. The sales process should be viewed as dynamic since business relationships change regularly."

•

"For the particular business I am in and the type of sales calls I have, I find that the books in the Pinpoint Sales Training Series are very often applicable to how I conduct business. I would recommend them to other sales people, just not ones that are in my industry."

•

"These books provide very good concepts. It fits in well with the Bell Leadership training program that I attended in November."

•

"I use this material in these books and apply it to my customers and other employees I work with."

•

"I would like to know other topics. Is there anything on Production Management or Consultative Selling or Time Management?"

•

"These books are great tools that should be used as guidelines for our everyday

supervisory practices. You need to take the time to do a short self-evaluation when reading them."

•

"The Pinpoint Training Series delivers information that could be used in a lot different areas."

•

"I like this because I can take them with me to read at a convenient time. I feel the little time I have to spend in the office is best use on activities that directly relate to revenue opportunities. I like the short amount of time it takes to keep up with these."

•

"I prefer the self-study approach; it fits in with my schedule."

•

"My thought is that the real value of these books comes into effect when doing the action plans."

•

"Short and sweet. These books are easy to comprehend."

•

"I have enjoyed reading these books. They are relevant to today's work environment and the ongoing change in the way we manage our workforce."

•

"I do feel that these books have been very helpful to me at my job."

•

"I think a lot of the recommendations in these books are very useful, and can be applicable to everyday situations. If nothing else, it's a good reference guide to fall back upon if a situation arises in the future."

•

"These books are relevant to today's work environment and the ongoing change in the way we manage our workforce."

•

Productive Sales Calling Strategies

Pinpoint Sales Skill Development Training Series

TIMOTHY F. BEDNARZ

MAJORIUM
BUSINESS PRESS

Pinpoint Sales Skill Development Training Series
"Productive Sales Calling Strategies"
Timothy F. Bednarz

Graphic design: Monika Pawlak

Majorium Business Press
2025 Main Street
Stevens Point, WI 54481
715.342.1018 • 800.654.4935

ISBN 978-1-882181-87-2

Printed in the United States of America

Introduction

The Pinpoint Sales Skill Development Training Series is designed for targeted training and education regarding increased improvement in a specific skill or competency.

Each book within this series is designed to be easy to use, understand and apply to your job. It can be used as a basis for training individuals, as a discussion guide or as a personal training tool.

Each chapter within this book discusses a specific concept. When you have completed all eight chapters you should have a 360° perspective of the topic.

Additionally, each chapter is divided into specific sections:

- The first section provides you with an overview of the topic
- The Implications section discusses why the concept is important, and why it is important to learn and apply.
- The Strategies, Tips & Techniques to Apply section teaches how to use and apply the particular concept to your work.
- The Points to Ponder section gives you something to think about or to be discussed with a group setting. These are questions not meant to be immediately answered, but to be pondered over time.
- The Training Activity section provides you with the tools to transfer what you have learned to your job. It is designed to help create an action plan to effectively apply the concept.

Each of the topics in this series is time-tested and proven in the marketplace. They have been used by thousands of employees as training tools. Many of the users have commented that what made these books valuable, was the ability to refer to them when a problem surfaced. They indicated that they remembered reading about the exact problem. They referred back to these books and found an appropriate solution.

You will find them equally valuable as a resource in your professional development library.

Table of Contents

LEARNING OBJECTIVES:

- The importance of planning and preparation in sales calling.
- To identify the structure of the sales call.
- To set call goals and objectives.
- To utilize effective sales call techniques.
- The problems and pitfalls associated with sales calls.
- To evaluate the success of a sales call.

1

Maximizing the Effectiveness of the Sales Call

It is often said that, "the devil is in the details." When salespeople fail to plan and prepare their sales calls, they have a tendency to become sloppy in their work habits. This sloppiness results in critical details being ignored or eliminated. This reduces the effectiveness of their calls and increases the likelihood of destroying the sale.

IMPLICATIONS — WHAT THIS MEANS TO YOU

Unfortunately many salespeople have the tendency to "wing it" on their sales calls. This is both ineffective and inefficient: each contact should have a purpose that is part of the master sales plan for each prospect. Salespeople should know precisely what they want to accomplish and should have each call outlined to realize their goals and objectives.

Salespeople only have a limited numbers of hours to devote to selling. The difference between exceptional and average salespeople lies in how that time is spent. Unplanned and unprepared sales calls can waste significant amounts of time and sap productivity. Every hour and every sales call must count and produce results for the salesperson and their company.

STRATEGIES, TIPS & TECHNIQUES TO APPLY

If salespeople are not making their calls with a clearly outlined purpose they are wasting both their own and their customers' time. Any call plan should include the following steps:

Goals and Objectives

Every sales call should have clearly defined goals and objectives. These should be prepared ahead of time and incorporated into the salesperson's weekly sales plan. In this manner any necessary research and preparation can be done ahead of time with the information at the salesperson's fingertips. Many salespeople will define their goals as they are walking through the prospect's door, but this is a haphazard approach to selling that will result in longer sales cycles and missed opportunities.

Opening Statement

During an initial sales call, the opening statement is critical to getting the prospect's attention and to sparking their interest. While this may not be as important in subsequent sales calls, a strong opening statement should be established for each call to set the tone and agenda for the meeting.

Questioning

A large portion of each sales call should be devoted to questioning and listening to the prospect. Salespeople will not be able to gather needs, identify problems, concerns and opportunities, or zero in on the prospect's pain or discontent if they do the majority of the talking. Astute salespeople use questions to move the sale forward and focus the prospect on what they have to offer. Additionally, when the prospect is allowed to do the majority of the talking they are made to feel important and that the salesperson is genuinely interested in what they have to say.

Presentation

The presentation portion of the sales call should be used to educate the prospect about the benefits the salesperson has to offer them. This is where testimonials and product demonstrations can be incorporated into the call.

It should be noted that, depending upon the selling style of the salesperson, in many instances the questioning and presentation phases might be handled together.

Closing

The closing portion of the sales call should be a summation of the activities and actions that have taken place during the call. This reinforces the call in the prospect's mind and should lead to the final stage of the contact.

Action

No sales call should conclude without a call for action. In many cases a trial close may be appropriate. Certainly after the prospect has been developed, a close should be employed where salespeople ask for the order.

Many salespeople are afraid to ask for the order out of fear that they will be denied and lose the business. However, being rebuffed does not equate to rejection. Persistent salespeople will recognize that this is often a signal that they need to educate the customer further before they ask for action again.

In all circumstances, each sales call should end with asking the prospect to commit to the next step, which may be another appointment, a product demonstration or a proposal. While it is up to the salesperson to define the next step, they should not leave the prospect's office or end the contact without mutual agreement as to the course of action.

POINTS TO PONDER – SOMETHING TO THINK ABOUT

1. What sequence or stages are you currently employing during your sales calls?
2. Do you plan your calls or do you have a tendency to "wing it"?

TRAINING ACTIVITY – APPLICATION & ACTION PLAN

1. Develop a plan for each of your sales call for the next two weeks using the following stages.
    - Goals and objectives
    - Opening statement
    - Questioning
    - Presentation
    - Closing
    - Action
2. Compare the results with the previous two weeks' sales calls.
3. Determine the changes and differences in results.

2

The Variables That Affect Sales Calls

Salespeople are competing for the customer's business on multiple levels. More importantly, they are competing for their time. As such, when making sales calls, there are a number of variables to be taken into account that have a significant impact on the success or failure of the call.

IMPLICATIONS — WHAT THIS MEANS TO YOU

In a perfect world, salespeople would be welcomed at every sales call and have the customers on the edge of their seat in rapt attention to everything they had to say to them. Unfortunately, sales calls are considered by most to be more of an interruption in a busy schedule than a welcome visit.

Many variables impact a sales call, most of which are out of the salesperson's control. However, it is important to recognize these variables and understand that rather than suffer through an unproductive call, it is better to reschedule when the timing is better. This demonstrates respect for the customer, their time and the demands placed upon them, which then often makes them more attentive on the next call. The alternative is to be brushed off by a frantic and harried manager with little chance of another appointment.

STRATEGIES, TIPS & TECHNIQUES TO APPLY

Whether contact is made face-to-face or over the telephone, there are a number of variables that can impact the success or failure of a particular sales call. It should be noted that these variables change from call to call.

Timing

Even when sales calls are scheduled, they may be poorly timed from the customer's perspective. They may feel obligated to meet with the salesperson, but with the demands placed upon them and the pressing issues and problems they must resolve immediately, their heart often isn't in the meeting. What the salesperson has to discuss may be important to the buyer, but their mind is on other matters.

In these circumstances, the salesperson should respect the buyer's time and realize that nothing of consequence will be decided under these circumstances. The salesperson is better served to cut the meeting short and ask to reschedule it. Most of the time the buyer will be thankful and willing to reschedule for a more convenient time.

Activity

In other situations, the salesperson may be in the middle of the sales call only to discover the buyer is distracted by activities and other disruptions outside of the office. Perhaps an emergency or other significant event is occurring, in which case this activity has their attention and the salesperson does not have the option of closing the door to keep the buyer focused. The salesperson should graciously indicate that a problem appears to exist and offer to reschedule for a more opportune time. If the problem is not serious, the buyer will often refocus their attention; otherwise, they will appreciate the opportunity to reschedule the appointment.

Attention

There may be times when the buyer is obviously inattentive and focused on other issues and problems. In this case the salesperson may offer to discuss the concerns. If the buyer is reluctant to do so, the salesperson should again offer to return at a time when they will be better able to consider what is being discussed.

Distractions

Salespeople often find themselves in circumstances when the buyer is distracted by numerous phone calls and interruptions. This can be an indication that the buyer is either very busy or using these disruptions to attempt to gain control over the situation. In other circumstances, buyers use distractions as an excuse to end the call and brush the salesperson off.

It is up to the salesperson to evaluate the situation and determine the proper course of action. If interruptions appear to be legitimate, they should offer to reschedule, perhaps for breakfast or lunch, in a neutral location where the buyer will not be distracted. If interruptions appear to be a ploy to dismiss the salesperson, one tactic is to directly ask for an undivided one or two minutes to clearly and concisely state several compelling reasons why the buyer should invest additional time to listen to what the salesperson has to say.

Interest

If the salesperson has failed to spark the buyer's interest with several compelling reasons to buy from him or her, they may use one or more of the variables listed in this lesson as an excuse to brush the salesperson off. This may be lost on the novice or unseasoned salesperson who views the reasons as legitimate.

POINTS TO PONDER — SOMETHING TO THINK ABOUT

1. Are you cognizant of the variables surrounding each sales call?
2. Do you have a tendency to keep selling regardless of poor timing or interruptions or do you stop and ask to reschedule for a better time?

TRAINING ACTIVITY — APPLICATION & ACTION PLAN

Listed below are five sales call variables:

- Timing
- Activity
- Attention
- Distractions
- Interest

1. Determine if there other variables that you may have experienced and add them to the list.
2. List specific situations you have encountered under each of the variables.
3. Identify the actions you took in each situation.
4. Determine whether in retrospect there may have been a better alternative to handling each situation.

3

Common Pitfalls and Problems Associated with Sales Calls

It is very easy for salespeople to fall into poor selling habits. During boom selling times, salespeople often eliminate many selling steps and techniques because they feel they are unnecessary. As the economy tightens up, these gaps in sales strategies become readily apparent and result in many selling problems.

IMPLICATIONS – WHAT THIS MEANS TO YOU

A well-executed sales call takes time and effort to plan and prepare for. Without a solid foundation of information, expertise and knowledge, it is extremely difficult for salespeople to be successful and maximize their results. This is where the majority of sales failures stem from. Buyers today are under a variety of increasing pressures to deliver effective solutions for their companies. They have little time or patience to talk with a poorly prepared salesperson, who they perceive has nothing of value to offer them.

Even if salespeople have the most effective product or service to sell, without proper preparation they will defeat themselves before they even start. Customers are seeking effective solutions and welcome the salesperson who can educate them about the value and benefits of the product or service they sell. The salesperson who fails to take the time to prepare and learn about the customer's business and use that knowledge to mutually explore the advantages his or her product can deliver to solve a problem or address an issue is squandering valuable time and opportunities.

STRATEGIES, TIPS & TECHNIQUES TO APPLY

Many salespeople fail to execute properly. They may have learned effective selling techniques, but over time have revised them into an approach they feel is more effective. Critical steps are eliminated as inefficient time-wasters, resulting in minimal results. In other cases, salespeople assume to know what is best for the prospect or customer. Consequently, many fall into most of the common pitfalls associated with sales calls, including:

'Winging It'

Many salespeople fail to see the need for record keeping and planning. Their business is "in their heads." Consequently, while a prospect or customer may be on their schedule, they fail to prepare and plan for the call. Instead, they wing it and see what happens.

There is a critical difference between scheduling and planning. Scheduling simply puts a call on the calendar; planning prepares for the call. Salespeople who schedule and then "wing it" are reactive and allow the prospect or customer to control the call and set the agenda.

Talking to the Wrong Person

Many salespeople confuse activity with results. Their rationale is that it doesn't matter who they are talking to—as long as they make the call, they are doing their job. They fail to understand that they are being paid to produce results, not create activity.

Talking with a non-decision maker is acceptable during an informational call, when salespeople are attempting to gather information and identify those with buying authority. After that, they need to focus their sales activities around the decision makers.

Talking Too Much

Overly eager to tell the customer about what they have to offer, many salespeople will dominate the conversation during the sales call. However, telling is not selling. The vast majority of each sales call should be devoted to open-ended questioning of the prospect or customer. Once the salesperson asks the question, he or she should quickly step outside of the conversation and allow the prospect or customer to talk. They should only reenter to ask additional questions to expand upon what the prospect or customer is saying.

Focusing on Nurturing

Many salespeople will state that the objective of their calls is to nurture the prospect or customer. However, nurturing is inadequate as a primary goal and objective, and wastes time when viewed as such. Each contact should be part of the overall sales plan for that account. Each should have a specific goal to move the sale one step closer. Nurturing is done within that context and should never be viewed as the sole objective of the call.

Failing to Control the Call

Salespeople who fail to plan and prepare for each appointment often surrender control of the call to the customer. Rather than move the sale forward, the customer dictates the objective of the call, which often leads the salesperson down blind, time-wasting alleys.

Selling Features Instead of Value-Added Solutions

Many salespeople believe they are selling a product or service rather than value-added solutions that solve problems or provide answers to pressing issues. The reality is no one buys a product or service; they buy what that product or service can do for them. It is up to the salesperson to first identify the customer's needs, then craft a solution that answers those needs.

Not Asking for the Order

At the end of every call salespeople should be asking either for the order or what is preventing the customer from moving ahead with the sale. In either case they will have either the order or the reasons why the customer is not yet ready to buy. This is a critical step that every salesperson must take before concluding the sales call. Failure to do so is a failure to fulfill one's basic responsibility as a salesperson.

Ending the Call Without a Commitment

If the prospect or customer is not yet ready to commit to the purchase, then before they conclude the call salespeople are obligated to get them to agree to the next action step. This may include another appointment, a presentation or a product demonstration. Whatever the next step, salespeople must gain the customer's commitment to move forward.

POINTS TO PONDER — SOMETHING TO THINK ABOUT

1. Do you ask for the order and inquire as to the reasons why the prospect or customer is not ready to buy at the end of every sales call?
2. Do you get the customer's commitment to the next step before ending each sales call?

TRAINING ACTIVITY — APPLICATION & ACTION PLAN

1. On a sheet of paper create a list of questions that you can use that leads the prospect or customer to a commitment including asking for the order or inquiring as to the reasons why they are not ready to buy.
2. Formulate a minimum of three or four variations of the same question that can be used repeatedly during the call.

4

Recovering from Poorly Executed Call Strategies

Poorly executed techniques and bad sales habits are difficult to break once they have become ingrained. It takes a conscious effort and consistent application of new and effective selling techniques over a prolonged period of time before the new can replace the old. With the personal desire and motivation to change and improve, salespeople should have the internal discipline to change their bad habits and replace them with more effective ones.

IMPLICATIONS — WHAT THIS MEANS TO YOU

Through repeated use, the salesperson's selling habits become ingrained over time. Good sales habits are continually reinforced by the results they produce, but so are the bad habits that result in frustration and anxiety. The problem often lies in the fact that without outside guidance and intervention, most salespeople are unaware of what constitutes a good and bad habit.

Every salesperson slips into bad habits. They may have eliminated steps to save time or used a technique that worked well in the past and expanded its use, but it has failed to work again.

Successful selling is not the result of fancy techniques and strategies, but the consistent application and execution of basic selling skills. The difference between a novice and a seasoned pro is in the execution of skills developed over time. When salespeople are experiencing selling problems and frustrations, they are best served not to let their personal pride interfere with their performance, and to discuss their problems with their managers in order to obtain an outside perspective.

STRATEGIES, TIPS & TECHNIQUES TO APPLY

Recovering from poor sales call techniques is not difficult, but often means salespeople must literally start over with the account and establish a firm foundation upon which to build the sale. Some of the prior information and work might be salvageable, but it is inadvisable to build the sale on these efforts.

Additionally, the biggest problem may lie with the prospect or customer. Up to this point, they may have felt the salesperson had little of value to offer and that talking to them only wasted their time. The salesperson must anticipate such a reaction and be prepared to counter it. If it persists, it will be extremely difficult to revive that account since the customer is reacting to initial negative perceptions created by the salesperson.

The following techniques are recommended in order to recover from poorly executed sales calls:

Develop a Call Plan

The first step in any recovery is to develop a call or account plan. Within this structure, salespeople must take the time to detail the specific information they have gathered about the prospect or customer. Once they have done this, they must analyze it and identify any gaps. Additionally, they must take the time to see if the information spotlights or pinpoints specific needs or hot-button issues that were previously ignored.

Based upon this information and analysis, the salesperson should develop a plan that details step-by-step and call-by-call how the customer can and will be sold. If there is resistance stemming from the failure of prior calls, the salesperson will need to anticipate this and determine how they will overcome it in order to get back in front of the customer.

Establish Objectives for Each Call

Within the structure of the call plan and prior to any sales call, specific goals and objectives should be established. Adequate planning and preparation should be devoted to developing questions, key points and the presentation required for each specific call. Ideally, a call sheet should be prepared with this information detailed on it that salespeople can refer to within the context of the call.

Re-Qualify

If poorly executed sales strategies were employed in the past, it is very likely that the customer was not properly qualified in the first place. Therefore it is of paramount importance that salespeople initially take the time to properly and adequately qualify the customer. This is not a step that can be minimized or eliminated: it determines the customer's needs, timing and priority of the prospect. Left undone, it will result in additional objections, stalls and problems later in the sale. Additionally, this procedure will reestablish the salesperson's credibility and clearly convey the message that the customer's business is both important and valued.

Salespeople should not announce that they are re-qualifying the customer or make a major issue of it, but should quietly start to ask questions that establish the customer's need and ability to buy as well as identifying key needs, problems or issues. When salespeople make an announcement that they made a mistake and now need to take the time to recover, they demonstrate a lack of polish and professionalism, and will likely be shown the door.

Utilize Information Gathering Techniques

Salespeople need to use information gathering techniques that pose the right open-ended questions in the proper sequence, so as to be non-threatening while developing key customer knowledge.

Link Benefits to Needs

No matter what they sell, salespeople must link their product's benefits to the customer's stated needs. Only in this fashion—addressing the precise areas that he or she has clearly stated is important to them—can they motivate the buyer. Without these linkages, the customer will not find what the salesperson has to say to be important. When presented with an area of interest, they will be motivated to learn more.

Advance the Sale Step-by-Step

Once the salesperson has reestablished him or herself, the final step is to follow the call plan and advance the sale, call-by-call. It becomes a simple exercise in execution.

POINTS TO PONDER — SOMETHING TO THINK ABOUT

1. How have you recovered from poorly executed sales calls in the past? Were your efforts effective?
2. Do you see the differences between a well and poorly executed sales call and why a well planned one can be more effective?

TRAINING ACTIVITY — APPLICATION & ACTION PLAN

1. A call sheet is a very useful sales tool that every salesperson should employ.
2. Design a sheet that you can use in a form that you will actually use. The following elements should be incorporated:
    - Call goal and objectives
    - What do you need to do?
    - What information needs to be gathered?
    - What information needs to be transmitted?
    - What specific questions do you need to ask and in what sequence?

- What action do you want the prospect or customer to commit to at the conclusion of the call?

3. Once designed, use these call sheets for a minimum of 30 days in order to make utilizing this sales tool a habit.

5

Effective Calling Strategies

Salespeople must understand the economics of selling their prospects and customers. There are a variety of calling methods that are cost effective in accomplishing contact goals and objectives. Not every sales call needs to be a face-to-face appointment, especially when the high costs of personal calls are factored into the equation.

IMPLICATIONS — WHAT THIS MEANS TO YOU

Since every sales call is part of an overall account plan, salespeople must determine the optimal mix of call methods and styles that will land the sale in the most cost effective manner.

Advances in technology have extended the salesperson's reach and effectiveness, and changed the face and complexion of selling itself. Salespeople have more communication options available that allow them to contact and maintain more accounts faster and more effectively than ever before. Successful salespeople learn to use available technology to increase their personal productivity and results.

STRATEGIES, TIPS & TECHNIQUES TO APPLY

For obvious reasons, not every sales call will be made in person. In fact, the personal visit represents a company's most costly sales contact. Rather than spend unnecessarily in this expensive area, salespeople should reserve the face-to-face call as a tool to make presentations at critical points in the sales process, or to negotiate or close the sale. Most of the other details of the sale can be taken care of with other more cost-effective calling methods. For this reason, in developing a calling plan for a specific prospect or customer, salespeople should create an effective mix of calling methods.

Type and Purpose

There are a variety of types of sales calls designed to fulfill specific objectives. These include:

Informational Call – An informational call is used to gather preliminary information about a company and to identify decision maker(s). Later in the sales process, an informational call is used to probe and question a prospect or customer about their needs, problems and concerns.

Qualifying Call – Used to qualify the prospect and to develop sufficient information to determine if there is a legitimate need for a product or service, the degree of that need and whether or not the prospect can afford the product.

Problem Solving Call – Used to solve specific problems and to smooth over any angry and hostile feelings the prospect or customer may have.

The Sales Presentation – The presentation call is used to make a formal sales presentation to a buyer or buying committee.

Demonstration Call – Used to conduct a product demonstration or trial.

Negotiation Call – Used to negotiate the terms of the deal and close the sale.

Service Call – The service call is used to follow up with the prospect or customer and to provide the service needed to ensure satisfaction.

Method

In addition to personal visits, the phone and mail, a number of newer contact options are available in email, webcasting and faxing. Every salesperson has developed their creative sales style and should explore the best mix of communication tools to maximize their sales effectiveness and impact. When asking a question, a quick email is often more effective than a phone call. In other situations, a phone call may be more effective than a personal visit. As salespeople create their call plans, they must determine the communication mix best suited to achieving the goals and objectives of each individual contact.

Frequency

The frequency of the sales call is dependent upon a number of variables. Ideally, frequency should be set in a way that allows the sale to move forward in an efficient and effective manner.

Workload Criteria

Sales managers specify to salespeople the workload criteria. These are the number of calls to be made on an account by size and sales potential. The smaller the account, in terms of volume and sales potential, the fewer calls that should be made. This ensures that salespeople are making effective use of their sales time.

Follow-Up

Timing is essential in selling. Some accounts will not be in a position to make an immediate purchase. As their budgets may not be approved for 6 to 12 months, in many circumstances it makes little economic sense to contact them until they are prepared to make a commitment. In these cases, salespeople may wish to schedule the sending of marketing and informational pieces on a regular basis to keep their name in front of the customer until the timing is right. This can be done by mail, fax or email.

POINTS TO PONDER — SOMETHING TO THINK ABOUT

1. How much thought have you given to effective sales call strategies?
2. Do you use an overall account calling plan or do you simply plan your calls from week-to-week?

TRAINING ACTIVITY — APPLICATION & ACTION PLAN

1. Create a prototype call plan that can be modified for any account.
2. Detail the following factors:
    - Number of Calls
    - Type and Purpose
    - Method
    - Frequency
    - Workload Criteria
    - Follow-Up

6

Triggering Events

Selling is a psychological chess match. Throughout the entire sales process, there are a number of triggering events signaling that a salesperson should act. Many are subtle and take time and experience to recognize, while others are more obvious and should be observable to even the most novice salesperson.

IMPLICATIONS — WHAT THIS MEANS TO YOU

It has often been said that everyone is selling something, all of the time. Even little children learn to sell their parents on the concept of getting a toy, going to McDonald's or staying up late. The point is that most humans learn from childhood how to manipulate others and motivate them to do something they want. They learn to sell themselves. In so doing, they learn the basic human psychological skills that salespeople then polish and build upon.

Most of the triggering events occurring during a sales call are subtle forms of behaviors learned in childhood. If salespeople can master the art of interpreting these psychological messages, they will be extremely effective in motivating and selling their customers.

STRATEGIES, TIPS & TECHNIQUES TO APPLY

Throughout the course of a day's calls or an entire calling sequence to an individual prospect or customer, salespeople will experience a series of triggering events.

Brush-Offs

Brush-offs most commonly occur during the initial sales call when the prospect's or customer's interest has not been sufficiently piqued. They fail to see the value of investing their time and energy with the salesperson and seek to quickly terminate the call. These dismissals normally take the form of, "I'm not interested," "I'm happy with my current supplier," or, "I don't have a need."

Salespeople can experience more subtle brush-offs later in the sales process when the prospect or customer desires to terminate the sales process, such as not answering or returning phone calls, making excuses for not making a decision or using trips and other projects as a reason for not moving forward.

Stalls

Stalls are used to stop the salesperson either because they are too aggressive and moving too quickly or because they haven't received enough information to proceed with the sale. The prospect may still be interested but is using the stall to gain control of the process and get some breathing room.

In other instances, the stall is used because prospects or customers have placed themselves in a box. They may have given the impression they are the decision maker, when, in fact, they have no buying authority. In all cases, salespeople need to use effective questioning techniques to probe for the underlying reasons behind the stall.

Objections

Prospects and customers will use objections for two distinct reasons, and salespeople need to develop the discernment to distinguish between them.

Initially, objections are a signal for the salesperson to stop. In most cases insufficient knowledge and information has been provided for the prospect to make an educated buying decision. They are being pressured to buy and therefore need to stop the process. If salespeople have taken the time to properly qualify the prospect and educate them concerning the value the product can provide, they will experience fewer of these types of objections.

The second type of objection is really a request for additional information. While they may appear to be objections, seasoned salespeople treat them as what they are. If salespeople treat them as serious objections, their responses can put the prospect or customer on the defensive and make them far more resistant to the sale. The key is to listen closely to what the customer is actually saying, and to respond carefully to it.

Cues

Throughout every sales call, prospects and customers are sending cues that are very subtle and difficult for the novice to read. Akin to "reading between the lines," it is often *how* an individual says something through their speed, tone and volume of speech, diction, posture and body language that must be interpreted. What remains unsaid is often as important as what is being said during the conversation.

Cues are there if the salesperson takes the time to look for them. Often seasoned salespeople become masters of automatically picking up on a customer's cues.

Buying Signals

Many salespeople lose sales simply because they fail to pick up on buying signals. Prospects and customers clearly indicate that they want to buy, but will not until the salesperson closes them by asking for their business. Salespeople not attuned to such signals will continue to sell themselves right out of a sale.

Buying signals can indicate an emotional decision to purchase, such as talking in terms indicating ownership. These may be statements about the benefits they will receive when the product is in use. Additionally, questions about details such as colors, volume, delivery, service, etc. can all be indicative of the customer's inclination to buy.

Many novice salespeople will not pick up on buying signals or, if they do, will fail to act on them. When salespeople hear or see a buying signal, they should automatically use a trial close, and if resistance is not encountered, move directly to a close.

POINTS TO PONDER — SOMETHING TO THINK ABOUT

1. How aware are you of the triggering events that transpire during your sales calls?
2. How carefully do you observe the subtleties of interaction between you and your customers?

TRAINING ACTIVITY — APPLICATION & ACTION PLAN

1. During the next two weeks, take careful notes of all customer conversations.
2. Make a conscious effort to look for the following triggering events:
    - Brush-Offs
    - Stalls
    - Objections
    - Cues
    - Buying Signals
3. When you observe any of these events, make a note of what it was and your response to it.
4. Perform post-sales critiques to review whether you missed any triggering events.
5. After two weeks review your sales diary to see if there is any commonality providing you cues to each triggering event.

7

A Goal for Every Call

Salespeople should understand that there is a substantial difference between scheduling a sales call and planning for the call. While some consider simply putting a call on their planner to be adequate preparation, every contact should be part of an overall account plan that moves the prospect or customer one step further along in the sales process.

IMPLICATIONS — WHAT THIS MEANS TO YOU

On its face, selling is a straightforward process: the salesperson develops a sales strategy to educate and convince a prospect or customer to buy their product. It gets more complicated when salespeople must apply that strategy over literally hundreds of prospects and customers. This is where planning and preparation become essential, as no salesperson can store enough information in their heads to sustain an efficient and productive flow of sales and results.

Salespeople are increasingly becoming data and information specialists. Without these skills, they cannot hope to be successful. The "old time" salesperson who managed accounts in their head is long gone. Selling has become more sophisticated in response to the needs of the buyer, and salespeople must employ all of the tools at their disposal to become effective and productive.

STRATEGIES, TIPS & TECHNIQUES TO APPLY

Every sales activity should be undertaken with a purpose. Nothing should be done randomly—least of all sales calls and contacts. Each should have a specific purpose as part of an overall account plan. Such a plan provides the salesperson with a roadmap to sell that account and develop its business.

Before each sales call, salespeople should question themselves as to what needs to be accomplished during the contact:

- What is the reason for and goal of this call?
- How does this call fit into the overall account plan?
- Who is the individual to be contacted?
- What actions do I want the buyer to take?
- What's in it for them?
- What supporting information do I need to help reach my objectives?
- What information will I be requesting?
- Who will have that information?
- What specific questions do I need to ask to get that information?
- Why should the customer provide me with that information?
- What do I need to do to motivate the buyer to take those actions?
- What commitment do I want the buyer to make during this call?

Sales calls and contacts should not be a hit-or-miss affair. It takes patience and persistence to make actual contact with today's buyers; they are under too much pressure and have too little time to devote to salespeople. Consequently, calls must be consistent and focused to maximize the contact time between salesperson and buyer. Each appointment must be used to move the buyer one step closer to the sale. This is where the application of the salesperson's expertise and experience must be clearly evident in the buyer's mind.

Additionally, salespeople must create linkages between one call and the other in the buyer's mind. Before moving on to the business of the call, salespeople must summarize what transpired previously and what the buyer agreed to. Before the call is concluded, the salesperson and buyer agree upon the actions of the next call, which then form the salesperson's starting point when that call takes place. Without these reminders, many buyers will forget what has transpired and progressed during previous calls. One sales call blends into another in their minds, and it is the responsibility of the salesperson to keep these facts clear in the buyer's mind.

POINTS TO PONDER — SOMETHING TO THINK ABOUT

1. How do you make sure that every sales call counts?
2. Do you make certain each sales call is part of an overall sales plan for each prospect or customer?

TRAINING ACTIVITY — APPLICATION & ACTION PLAN

1. Examine your call plan for the upcoming week.
2. Identify how each specific sales call and contact fits into the overall account plan for each customer.
3. All calls without a defined purpose should be redefined or rescheduled.

8

The Post-Call Evaluation

Salespeople who take the time to plan and prepare for their sales calls need a method of monitoring and measuring the results of their activities. This gives them the ability to gauge their success and polish their selling skills. Everything salespeople do should be viewed as a learning experience, and every sales call as an opportunity to try a new technique or polish an old one.

IMPLICATIONS – WHAT THIS MEANS TO YOU

Successful salespeople are those who take the time to learn from their failures and mistakes through personal introspection and an honest self-assessment of their abilities. Accordingly, those who repeatedly make the same mistakes and poorly execute their sales strategies would benefit significantly from the use of post-sales call critiques. With the ability to evaluate their mistakes and failures and apply those lessons to future activities, salespeople vastly improve their odds of success.

STRATEGIES, TIPS & TECHNIQUES TO APPLY

Salespeople should conduct a formal sales critique after each call. Many salespeople mull over their calls, second-guessing the strategies they used and thinking about the key points they failed to emphasize, but it is also important to do this in a written and formal fashion. A disciplined approach to post-sales call assessments provides salespeople a means by which to learn from their mistakes, polish their skills and move forward.

Salespeople should create a simple questionnaire, then take a few moments immediately after each call or contact to complete it. In this way the call is still fresh in their memory and both the positive and negative aspects of the contact can be highlighted and focused upon.

A sample post-call questionnaire can include the following questions:

1. Did the sales call meet the stated goals and objectives?
2. What was done right?
3. Which key points did the prospect or customer respond positively to? Negatively?
4. What if any major mistakes were made?
5. If I had it to do over again, what would I change?
6. What were the key lessons learned from this call?
7. What do I need to do differently in the future?

Once salespeople have conducted a formal post-call critique, they should make notes to remedy the problems identified, and then forget they happened. It is essential that salespeople learn from their failures, forget they happened and dwell on the positive aspects of the call. Focusing on mistakes only creates doubt and anxiety over events that have already transpired and cannot be repeated.

It is recommended that salespeople continue to build their presentation on those aspects of their calls that prospects and customers responded positively to. As these points will tend to be the "hot-button" issues other prospects will also respond to, they need to be highlighted and focused on.

Salespeople should keep their questionnaires in a folder and conduct a regular weekly and monthly critique of all of their calls. A consistent follow-up will pinpoint weak areas in need of strengthening and remind salespeople of what has worked effectively. Done regularly, this will create a learning habit that polishes their skills and enhances their overall sales performance. The personal motivation to create this habit is one's personal desire to improve and produce additional results and commissions.

POINTS TO PONDER — SOMETHING TO THINK ABOUT

1. Do you conduct any type of formal review of your sales calls? Explain.
2. Are there lessons you feel you can learn by reviewing your performance during past sales calls?

TRAINING ACTIVITY — APPLICATION & ACTION PLAN

1. Develop a post-sales call critique for yourself.
2. Make copies of the critique available after each call.
3. Conduct a post-sales call critique.
4. Review your critiques weekly.
5. Do this for the next 30 days.

About the Author

Timothy F. Bednarz, Ph.D. is CEO of the American Management Development Group, Inc. For over 20 years he has researched, designed and authored hundreds of learning and development programs used by Fortune 1000 companies.

He is also the author of *Great! What Makes Leaders Great. What They Did, How They Did It and What You Can Learn from It* (2011).

Speaking Availability

Timothy F. Bednarz, Ph.D. is available for speaking engagements for your next meeting or association event. He can be contacted at 800-654-4935 or by e-mail at timothy.bednarz@majorium.com.

Bulk Sales

Bulk sales of this book or any other titles available from Majorium Business Press. Inquiries can be directed to sales@majorium.com, or by phone at 800-6654-4935.

Quick Order Form

Fax orders: 715-342-1118. Send this form.

Telephone orders: Call 800-654-4935 toll-free. Have your credit card ready.

Email orders: sales@majorium.com

Postal orders: Majorium Business Press, 2025 Main Street, Stevens Point, WI 54481, USA.

Please send the following books:

____

____

____

____

Please send more FREE information on:

☐Catalog ☐Speaking/Seminars ☐Mailing Lists ☐Consulting

Name: ____________________________________

Address: __________________________________

City: ____________________ State: _____ Zip: __________

Telephone: ________________________________

Email address: ______________________________

Sales tax: Please add 5.5% for products shipped to Wisconsin addresses.

Shipping by air:

United States: $4.00 for first book and $2.00 for each additional product.

International: $9.00 for first book; $5.00 for each additional product (estimate).

Made in United States
Cleveland, OH
06 November 2026

47678348R10026